This book is dedicated first to my husband, Ron, who is my best friend, my biggest supporter, and my most powerful accountability partner.
Without your love, your generous gift of time, and your encouragement, this book would not have been written.

Next, I dedicate this book to Samurai Camp 32:
Kimberley, Krystal, Paul and Tim
Trudy, Dan, Danielle, and Michael
Beth, Candy, Erin, Joe, Joshua, Kathy, Kristie, Ricardo, and Richard
And Aaron, Cathy & Mairi and the entire Team.
I love you all and I need your love.

Finally, I dedicate this book to the courageous individuals who were willing to be vulnerable, gut-level honest, and courageous in telling their stories.
Your names have been changed and your organizations disguised, but your stories are real and true and by telling them you are making a difference in countless lives. You have cast the pebble that creates the expanding ripples in the still pool, and for that I thank you from the bottom of my heart.

INTRODUCTION

"Stress leave" is now the number one reason for workplace absence due to illness or disability in Canada according to the Canadian Federation for Independent Business. These stress-related absences average 20 days in length and cost the economy almost five billion dollars a year. In the United States, according to the National Institute for Occupational Safety and Health (NIOSH), 40% of workers report their job is very or extremely stressful and 25% view their job as the number one stressor in their lives. Job stress is more strongly associated with health complaints than financial or family problems.

Workplace stress is caused by a number of factors, chief among them a combination of high demands and pressures coupled with a sense of having little control over those demands. Employment insecurity and fear of job less are also major factors. Yet, there's one underlying factor that's even more insidious and damaging – the toxic workplace.

What is a toxic workplace?

Wikipedia tells us that a toxic workplace is one marked by significant drama and infighting, the result of workers motivated by personal gain who use unethical and mean-spirited means to manipulate those around them, creating an environment that negatively impacts the viability of the organization.

While a toxic workplace may manifest in these ways, I suggest that it arises from a deeper place – a sense of disconnection from ourselves and from each other profound enough to allow damaging gossip, the formation of cliques with insiders and outsiders, mind games and other forms of manipulation, abusive treatment, lack of empathy and compassion, bullying, and even violence in the workplace.

Imagine waking up every morning knowing that you are heading to a workplace where your mental, emotional, physical, and spiritual health are at risk, or are already compromised. Where you put on your virtual suit of armour to protect yourself. Where you feel alone, isolated, powerless, choiceless. Where you trust no one. Where no one trusts you. Millions of North Americans live this reality daily. In the pages that follow, you'll meet some of them. Good people who have survived or are surviving bad circumstances, toxic workplaces. Their names have been changed and their organizations disguised, so that they could speak honestly, in safety.

And, following each of their stories, an analysis of what might actually be going on and action steps that can be taken in similar situations. Find what resonates for you – what speaks to your heart. Then, take action. Reclaim your life, your health, your soul.

Contents

Diana's Story

I used to steel myself to pick up the phone or walk into my boss's office for a meeting. My stomach hurt most of the time, and my jaw was permanently clenched. There was no respite – I was tied to my phone and email evenings, weekends, even while I was supposed to be on vacation. And I had to be "on" all the time – on top of everything, every minor detail. I remember watching that Bradley Cooper movie, "Limitless", and thinking that's him – that's my boss. Brilliant mind, unlimited capacity for detail, and not a shred of humanity to be found.

I guess I should have paid more attention as early as our first meeting, when I felt like I'd just been interrogated rather than interviewed. After all, most people behave better when interviewing candidates than they do in real life, right? I think part of me was flattered when he offered me the job – I felt like I'd passed a test, proved how smart I was. I didn't think about having to pass that test over and over and over again, every day for two years.

That's what it felt like – a test, every day. Several times a day actually. The question out of the blue, or the last minute assignment. The early morning or late night call with an expectation I'd answer and be ready to work. The constant probing, testing, questioning, and never knowing if I was passing the test. It made me start to second-guess myself.

Worse, I let it get to me in other ways. I was never in the here and now at home. Life went on in our house and I only half paid attention to my husband, our kids. At least half of me was always at work, even when I wasn't. I was on high alert all the time – and after a while, I actually forgot how to relax. Everything was urgent. Every detail mattered, at least at work. I became equally demanding of my staff, at least during the work day.

And then, just when I was actually feeling on top of things, the hammer dropped. I think he did it intentionally, that it was just my turn, like a game of roulette with the ball dropping on me. He wanted a status update. The call started out ok and then suddenly it was like something shifted. Suddenly he was yelling at me, tearing a strip off me. I don't even remember what he was angry about, just that it didn't seem important enough to provoke that kind of cold, laser-like rage.

I felt like I'd been punched in the stomach. I could barely breathe. My eyes were tearing up and I was working so hard at not crying, at controlling my voice. I knew he could hear how upset I was, but it didn't make a difference. He just kept hammering away at me, asking the same questions over and over again. I just kept praying for it to be over. It felt like an assault.

When it was finally over, I was shaken to the core. I felt stupid, incompetent, incapable. I cried most of the way back to the office. At some point it hit me that he was wrong. That I am smart, and capable, and competent. I remember yelling that over and over again in my car. I think that's what helped me pull myself together enough to go back to work.

He never apologized, or in any way overtly acknowledged what had happened. A few days later he invited me to lunch with some colleagues. I still felt lousy – lunch was the last thing I wanted to do. He was insistent, though, so I went and it was fine. Later I figured out that this was his way of acknowledging he'd lost it without ever having to say so.

I can't say I forgave or forgot. That first blow-up was always at the back of my mind, and the possibility of a repetition kept me on edge. I was wary of a repeat and it did eventually happen – and it wasn't any easier to get through than the first time but this time it just made be angry and resentful. By that time I'd had a quiet conversation with my predecessor, one of the most capable and together women I've ever worked with. When she opened up and told me she'd regularly broken down and cried while working for him, I knew it wasn't me. And we weren't alone – I could see the effect he had on the men who worked for him in meetings. His team meetings were the quietest meetings I'd ever attended. Everyone was dead serious. No one spoke unless asked a question. People with brilliant ideas didn't share them. It was completely dysfunctional.

And yet, what do you with it when the boss is a sociopath but he's a senior executive and widely considered to be high potential enough to have his eye on the corner office? I didn't complain. I didn't even tell the truth when I had the opportunity to – it felt too dangerous at the time. I waited for the chance to move into another job without looking like I was trying to get away from him. A year or so later he left the organization. It's funny because I had mixed feelings.

He was a monster to work for and I made such bad choices during that two years. On the other hand, I was never sharper, never more on top of my work, never more productive and effective than that time, working for him. I made bad choices to prove I was smart enough, and I did. I paid a huge cost, though. When I ask myself if I'd do it all over again … I have no answer. Or maybe I just don't want to admit, even to myself, that I would. And part of me adds "but on different terms", but I know that's not true. I'd do it all over again because of my addiction to being recognized for doing the impossible. My addiction to achievement. Plus, *how much greater is the recognition when it's coming from someone with impossibly high standards? The adrenalin rushes and the high of being recognized outweighed the exhaustion, the constant anxiety, the moments of panic, the cost to my health, my marriage, my kids ... I guess that's why heroin addicts keep using.*

Like many high achievers, Diana was drawn to a fellow high achiever and to the opportunity to excel. The almost irresistible lure of impressing the hard-to-impress can work as a trap, drawing some high achievers further and further in, until they can see no way out. The adrenaline high of success is short-lived, but addictive. And the pain of the failure – real or imagined – only feeds a desire for redemption. An effective manager can find an employee with an addiction to difficult successes a challenge to manage, particularly in the lows. What often appears to others as a minor setback can feel like an epic failure to the individual accustomed to succeeding. The opportunity to learn something and move on can be lost as the high achiever struggles with deeper questions of self-worth and worthiness.

On the other hand, for the manager who seeks control over his or her employees, this type of high achiever offers endless opportunities for manipulation. He or she requires little in the way of motivation, being internally motivated by the desire for favour and, equally, the fear of failure. They virtually never give up but will fight through almost any obstacle to achieve the goal and, even more importantly, what the goal represents – acceptance, recognition, validation. While providing these in good measure when success is reached is effective, an even more effective way to keep this type of high achiever pushing their limits is to withhold or temper them. For every near-impossible success, point out the one element that wasn't reached or wasn't perfect. Always find a flaw, no matter how minor, to incorporate into the positive feedback – "That was almost perfect, Diana – it's just too bad you didn't manage to do it faster."

For some period, Diana will try that much harder each time. If it was speed of execution the last time, she'll do it faster next time. If it was a budget issue, she'll underspend. The toxic element in this dysfunctional relationship is that the target's always moving. The success is never quite enough and the criteria for success shift each time. The high achiever remains off-balance, struggling to get it right and never quite succeeding until exhaustion, cynicism and disengagement set in. For the truly toxic manager, each stage of this "game" is a new set of opportunities to play with someone's mind while driving significant results. Ultimately the high achiever can no longer produce the results, of course, and they're replaced with a fresh new achiever.

Part and parcel of keeping someone is unbalanced is the qualified praise for successes interspersed with unqualified and merciless abuse for failure, real or imagined. With a team of high achievers, the verbal abuse can be rotated among them, keeping the entire team off balance. In some cases, relationships among team members deteriorate, particularly where the manager actively pits them against each other. In other cases, team members may offer each other quiet support and comfort. In even rarer situations, team members may band together to approach higher management for help with the toxic manager.

The challenge is often that high achievers have high expectations of themselves and others, including sometimes unreasonable expectations of being able to manage difficult behaviours. "The boss was hard on me today but I deserved it – I missed that deadline, after all – and I shouldn't be such a baby. He's hard on everyone and I should be able to take it." The more often we're exposed to these toxic behaviours, the more normal they become and the more we might expect to be able to tolerate them. Yet verbally abusive behaviour is not normal – no matter how often it might occur – but it is toxic. Over time, it erodes our resilience and we lose perspective. It's not unusual for those like Diana to leave a toxic situation burnt out, exhausted, and gun-shy.

Strategies for high achievers to avoid entrapping themselves in "the success vortex" start with self-awareness. Understanding ourselves deeply equips us to identify what draws us and why. Knowing we want to please those who are hard to please is a great red flag when considering a next job or a next assignment. Realizing how irresistible the adrenaline rush of the impossible project can be for us allows us to assess the pros and cons of an opportunity more realistically – including the risk to our own health and welfare.

We may decide to turn a job down – or we may intentionally structure a framework to support ourselves from becoming wholly swallowed up in a toxic situation. For example, we may engage a coach to hold us accountable to a pre-defined standard of mental and emotional self-care, hire a personal trainer to ensure we take care of our physical selves properly, and join a meditation group to ensure our spiritual wellbeing through the project. We may also create competing commitments for ourselves to maintain a healthier degree of equilibrium – for example, enrolling in a post-graduate degree program like an MBA ensures we maintain some focus outside of work as well as giving us a second powerful opportunity for achievement. For some, athletic pursuits serve the same function. In some cases, it's circumstances beyond our control that create the space we need from work, such as an aging parent or ailing child or spouse. These are circumstances, however, that carry their own stresses and can also in some cases channel us back toward work – if our pain on the home front is too great, work, even when toxic, can be a way of escaping.

Once we're entangled in this type of toxic workplace, where we'll do virtually anything to gain the praise and recognition of an overly-demanding manager, it can be extremely difficult to extricate ourselves. Giving up or admitting defeat is not in our DNA. Quitting a challenging situation feels like the ultimate failure. We might tell ourselves we'll quit as soon as we accomplish the next big milestone – leave on a high note. Yet we're unlikely to leave at a point when we're enjoying the gratification and rewards of success. Most often we leave these situations either at the point of burnout or for a new and even more challenging opportunity. Hence, identifying a potentially toxic situation upfront is doubly important.

Looking for clues is important and yet too often we screen out information we're picking up because we don't want to see it. Diana's interview experience completely foreshadowed her work experience, yet she chose to ignore it. If you see yourself in Diana, consider enrolling an accountability partner the next time you're interviewing –

someone to challenge your thinking and offer an alternative perspective. Ideally someone with a natural curiosity, rather than judgment, who knows you well enough to recognize high risk clues and ask the tough questions.

Finally, if you recognize yourself in Diana, you may want to do some work on yourself. Therapy, coaching, experiential seminars ... there are a myriad of ways to transform fear-based and unbalanced drivers of success to healthy and productive motivators.

Jane's Story

I felt like I was only ever as good as yesterday's numbers.

And even that wasn't enough – the bar kept rising, shifting. If we met the numbers, then they'd focus elsewhere, find something to criticize. There was rarely any appreciation or recognition for what we accomplished, only unrelenting pressure to do more, and nitpicking on anything that wasn't perfect.

The pressure was relentless. I'd accepted the job with the large health organization because it was a promotion and the recognition felt good. I also thought I'd have more control, giving me the ability to fix the processes and inefficiencies that were getting in the way in my previous role. I stayed because my family needed the paycheque. My husband didn't understand what it was like for me at work. He was afraid I'd quit and we were both afraid of what would happen to our family without my salary. I was being well compensated for my age and level of experience at the time and I didn't believe I could do as well elsewhere. And, truthfully, despite the long hours and heavy workload, I got to do a lot of interesting work – big projects that someone with my level of experience at the time wouldn't normally get to do.

Besides, I didn't have enough life experience in my early thirties to know – or even be able to hope or believe – that it could be any different elsewhere. This is what senior management was like everywhere, I thought – unrelenting pressure to perform in a thankless environment, and with an ever-expanding workload eating into my family time as I missed my children's events and activities, went back to work in the evening after supper, kept running on that treadmill. It all needed to look a certain way and that kept me going, running myself ragged, becoming frustrated and angry much of the time.

The people who reported to me were hurting too. It started as simply being on edge, particularly around Board meeting time. What began as being a little snippy with each other soon turned ugly and painful. They too went into survival mode and, as a team, it became a game of survival of the fittest, reporting on each other for the smallest of perceived infractions. None of my efforts to reassure them, to motivate them and keep their morale up, had any lasting effect. Not when the top leadership repeatedly made threats of changing the business model and eliminating all of our jobs. We were all living in a constant state of uncertainty, off balance and running hard to try and make it work.

And then I injured myself, working out. I quickly found that my prescription painkillers, when taken in excess of the prescribed dose, not only took my physical pain away but made everything else more bearable too. When I had enough in my system, it took the edge off the endless committee meetings, the brutal monthly board meetings, the worsening situation with my staff. When I look back at that time, I see myself standing in my office, in my elegant and professional business suit, a successful senior manager, pouring painkillers out onto my desk to count them so I knew how many I had and how many I had to figure out how to get.

Ultimately, of course, it got bad. Bad enough to confide in my husband and one of my girlfriends. Although they didn't understand how I could have gotten to that point, they were there for me. They helped me get off the pills. They helped me through some bad medical advice that actually made things worse before they got better. They even helped me through a hellish long weekend of withdrawal. And then my husband came to work with me and talked to my manager, who agreed to put me on a paid leave so I could get good medical care and regain my health. And when I did and I had my medical authorization to return to work, my job was gone. They'd finally implemented the restructuring they'd been threatening for years.

The six years of my life I spent in that organization, including the four in that role, taught me a lot about myself and the ways in which I can let myself off the hook. The process of getting out of that situation also gave my husband and I an opportunity to learn how to really communicate to come to a solution that works for both of us, to learn what each of us needs from the other to feel safe and secure, and to design our life together. And I've used the experience, empathy, and compassion I developed through surviving that workplace throughout my life and particularly in management roles I've had since then. While I never would have seen it this way at the time, that experience was one of my biggest blessings.

How many of us quietly relate to elements of Jane's story? Perhaps it's the trade-off of the big promotion and the big salary in return for all of our time and energy – particularly at an age and stage of our life when many of us are building our careers, buying homes we can barely afford, raising families, wanting it all to look as good as the proverbial Joneses. Perhaps it's the relentless pressure to produce bigger and better, the constantly shifting sands of performance expectations.

Perhaps it's the leadership culture of focusing on what wasn't accomplished, overlooking what's been created. Or the dog-eat-dog dynamic that develops among employees when sustained uncertainty and job insecurity becomes leadership's weapon of choice. Or perhaps it's the "escape-in-place": it doesn't have to be a full-blown addiction, it can look a lot of different ways. How many of us have an extra drink or two in the evening, or numb ourselves in our "spare time" with binge-watching Netflix series, or stuff our frustrations down our throat with that extra helping at dinner or the late night snacking?

And how many of us believe deep down in our hearts that this is how it is everywhere. That there is no real escape. That if we want the big bucks, this is the price we have to pay. Or even that we're inadequate – after all, if this is what it's like everywhere, then our brother-in-law who seems so happy, relaxed, and successful must just be far better at dealing with it than we are. And the woman who lives next door who leaves for her executive job before the sun is up and returns just in time to kiss her children good night and still finds time to chair the local community fundraiser – she's clearly a more capable individual than we are, right?

Jane's story combines all of the elements of a perfect storm, elements which in isolation of each other may or may not be harmful, and can even be healthy.

"What have you done for us lately?"

Focusing on results is an effective way to motivate ourselves to stretch our comfort zones, to take bold action, and to change the circumstances that may be holding us back. Those circumstances may be unwieldy, bureaucratic procedures, an outdated way of looking at our customers or marketplace, the tools we're using, or any number of factors external to us. When we're looking past the perceived obstacles to a clear vision of what success looks like, we're driven to achieve and our creative juices start to flow. We can open ourselves up to possibility thinking, finding new and creative ways to move forward. We can even have fun creating the results we're going after!

The joy of creating and achieving is sustained through encouragement, recognition, and celebration. When our successes are overlooked or taken for granted – "after all, that's your job, isn't it?" – we can feel deflated and unappreciated. Over time, a feeling of not being appreciated can easily become a sense of not being valued, which is not only deeper and more hurtful, but also feeds any inner sense of lack of self-worth from which we might already suffer. Many of us struggle with self-doubt and feelings of unworthiness throughout our lives. When our environment at home and/or at work sends us subtle (or not so subtle) messages that reinforce those deep-seated and often unconscious beliefs, we can easily shift to a fight, flight, or freeze modality.

Fight tends to manifest in the workplace as resistance, confrontation, or passive aggression. The supervisor who often seems frustrated or angry. The colleague who fights every change, seemingly just to be difficult. The people who nod and smile during the meeting, seemingly in agreement with a path forward, who then passively or actively sabotage it. Flight can be seen in those who are constantly looking for the next job, whether within their organization or outside. Flight can also be the escape-in-place that takes the edge off and allows the individual to stay and perform, but at a personal cost that tends to increase over time. Freeze may be even more damaging, as people become stuck – unable to move out, unable to perform, surviving each day with a sense of quiet desperation while waiting to be found out and punished.

How different does it look when results are recognized and celebrated? When the dedication, creativity, and effort required to accomplish those results is acknowledged and rewarded? When we take time out from our busy workdays to affirm everyone on the team that accomplished the result? When results and achievement sustained over time are rewarded in tangible and intangible ways? When failure is not seized as an opportunity for blame and punishment, but treated as an opportunity to learn, to acknowledge what went right, and to let go and move forward?

"What have you done for us lately" only requires a minor shift to create healthy results – imagine a supervisor who regularly starts a conversation with "Here's what you have done for us lately" and goes on to list accomplishments and contributions. What would that workplace be like? What would that organization achieve?

Think about how much more breathing space Jane would have had if her efforts and results had been acknowledged, or even celebrated. Had she been encouraged – or perhaps even at a minimum had she not been actively discouraged - her motivation might have come from a place of positivity and possibility, fueling rather than depleting her. She might have allowed herself an occasional break to attend one of her children's milestone activities. She might have been able to offer genuine reassurance and comfort to her staff, short-circuiting some of their stress behaviours. She might have avoided the addiction to painkillers and found healthier, easier ways to learn the lessons of self-worth, communication, and empathy.

"Let's focus on where you missed the mark – all the things you did wrong or didn't get to at all"

Learning from what didn't work is effective. When we take the time to understand why we didn't accomplish what we said we would, we learn about ourselves – our level of commitment, what else might have been more important to us, where we let ourselves off the hook, where we could have asked for support and chose not to (and why), and more. That exploration can be incredibly valuable to us if we choose to apply those learnings going forward. Even with acknowledgment and celebration of achievement, however, moving to learning from what didn't work is tricky.

Many of us tend to focus on the negative. Have you ever read a performance review or a 360 degree feedback report and had to read it two or three times before seeing any of the positive comments, for example? Or focusing on the one opportunity for improvement and not the three or four or more acknowledgments in the last conversation with our manager? Our minds seem to be programmed to quickly identify what's not working and to glide over what is working.

Creating the potentially huge value of learning what didn't work is, therefore, a careful exercise. Ideally it starts with acknowledgement of successes and wraps up with acknowledgments of the value of the learnings. In between, it's most effective if we are encouraged to answer that question for ourselves, rather than being told what didn't work, and if whoever's doing the asking is able to probe, gently and with open-ended questions. Creating a safe environment and coming from an intention of genuinely supporting and being curious is key.

In Jane's situation, the Board of Directors not only barely acknowledged the results achieved, but actively focused on what didn't work. The experience of being told where she and the team had failed, sometimes in relatively minor ways, month after month, and in a spirit of criticism rather than curiosity and support, felt like a relentless attack. Imagine the ways in which Jane must have had to prepare herself for that monthly meeting, her neat and professional business suit ironically symbolizing the mental and emotional suit of armour needed to get through that meeting without cracking.

How different could it have been if the Board had invested the time to ask Jane and her colleagues what support they need from the Board, where lack of tools might be holding them back, or whether they personally felt that they were set up for success?

"It's like this everywhere. If I want a senior role and all that goes with it, I need to play by the rules."

Perhaps most insidious of all is the belief that we have no choice. That there's a price to be paid for professional success. That professional success has to look a certain way.

I often hear managers of a certain age range (for the record, mine), express a view that young workers who are relatively new to the workforce are not interested in "paying their dues". That they're an entitled bunch, expecting money, promotions, and perquisites to be handed to them without the kind of effort we put in to climb the corporate ladder. When I look back at the choices I made during that climb, I confess a secret hope that my own children won't make the same choices. That their generation will rebel against the mantras of bottom-line results, raising the bar, doing more with less, paying their dues. And that this rebellion, this outright refusal to conform, comply, submit, will create a revolution in the corporate world, re-humanizing it.

We owe our employers our best effort. To me, that means the best we can do at any given time – our creativity, our intellect, our passionate contribution, our collaboration and teamwork. We don't, however, owe them our soul. We don't owe them every waking hour of our lives, the sacrifice of our family commitments, or every last ounce of our energy. We don't owe them blind obedience, compliance with patently unreasonable rules and requests, or the fortitude to sit through dehumanizing conversations.

Jane, like many of us, put her job before everything else. Before her family, before her community, and, most damagingly, before herself. She sacrificed it all – mental, physical, and emotional health and well-being, a sustainable balance or equilibrium in her life, and the moments with her children which can never be recovered. Whatever financial recompense Jane received, it could not have been enough.

It's easy to buy the common wisdom that "it's like this everywhere". Yet we owe it to ourselves to explore that. A quick internet search yields page upon page of results for successful and thriving organizations with a different, people-centred ethos. Not because they don't care about results, but because they do. Results achieved through unrelenting pressure, fear-mongering, and deliberately creating or unintentionally maintaining uncertainty and instability, aren't sustainable in the longer-term. Human beings have a breaking point, whether that moment is at the extreme end manifesting in workplace violence, or a quiet decision to check out and leave - or an even worse decision to check out and stay.

How different would our organizations be if we actively encouraged each other to seek equilibrium – to balance those periods of intense work activity, long hours, and singular focus to achieve some result, with periods during which we recharge our batteries, share learnings, reduce our time and effort? How much more effective would both organizations and people be if we clearly distinguished between important priorities and the rest? If we rewarded people for results against those few important priorities rather than creating environments where "face time" matters more?

What can we do differently?

As leaders in organizations, we can:

- Take the time to understand the level of effort required to achieve results so that we can acknowledge the contribution – and the sacrifices – our people are making.

- Acknowledge, recognize, and celebrate achievements – large and small – so that our people feel seen and valued. Pay particular attention to and highlight results created without heroic sacrifices – encourage healthy, sustainable work habits even while focusing on results.

- Identify high priority results and activities – when "everything" is important, either nothing is or we run a risk of burning people out.

- Pay attention to our people and their wellbeing – watch for changes in manner or behaviour. Get curious when we see new behaviours. If a normally even-tempered, laid-back individual starts to exhibit repeated signs of irritability and frustration, for example, get curious. It may be that he has a new baby at home and isn't getting much sleep, or he may be worried about completing a high priority project at work on time and within budget. Either way, he could use our support. Equally, the normally passionately engaged employee who's suddenly gone quiet in meetings, the exuberant morning person who's showing up late for work, and the single mom who's started working late into the evening deserves our time and attention.

- Know what motivates our people and know what demotivates them. How? By asking them.

- Ask regularly what support people need – normalize the idea that no one is an island, that we're all in it together, and that's it okay to ask for support.

- Create safe opportunities for people to share learnings and insights – one employee's shared self-discovery that they could have achieved a different result by asking for help earlier creates a space for others to ask for that help when they need it.

- Model effective workplace behaviours – from respect, encouragement, and acknowledgment, to working reasonable hours, taking our vacation time, avoiding late night emails (even if we don't expect them to be acknowledged or answered until the next day). People look for evidence – they watch what we do and replicate it, rather than listening to what we say. All the messages in the world about valuing work/life balance mean nothing if we're putting in long hours and ignoring our non-work commitments on an ongoing basis.
- Create opportunities for flexible working hours, compressed work weeks, remote work, and other ways to reduce stress created by lengthy commutes, daycare deadlines, and other hazards of today's world.

As employees, we can:

- Be honest with ourselves and take ownership for our choices. There are times in our life and in our career when we intentionally choose high pressure, high reward work assignments in dysfunctional or toxic workplaces. Whether that's an effective choice or not is something we get to look at – but we can't do that until we own our choice.

- Look for possibilities even where we don't believe they exist. There's always another choice. We may not like the consequences or costs of that choice, but we get to look at whether they're truly greater than the choice we're making. Leaving a toxic workplace has short-term costs and risks which we can weigh against the short and longer-term benefits if we're willing to accept that we have choices.

- Ask for what we need or want without assuming we can't have it. Often we limit our own possibilities by deciding in advance that if we asked for more flexible working hours or an extension of a deadline that the answer will be no. Sometimes it is. Other times we might be surprised with a yes, particularly if we've gone to the effort of enrolling the decision-maker by helping them see what's in it for them rather than focusing on what we want.

- Take responsibility for our own well-being. That means making the time to take care of ourselves. It also means doing an ongoing honest assessment of where we're at. It's easy to hide from the truth, to participate in the numbing activity of our choice without being intentional or even conscious of it. To deny the truth of it. That's a road that leads to places we might not want to end up, or we might even already be far down that road. Today's a good day to take stock and re-assess what's important to us.

- We can also take stock of our values – those most deeply held and deeply cherished ideals which, when we live in alignment with them create a sense of peace and harmony, and when we are out of alignment create a dissonance that ripples through every aspect of our lives. Make a list of your values and then do an honest assessment of which ones you're living out. For those you aren't, what do you want to do about it?

- Be radically honest when we're in a situation that we can't influence enough to detoxify it for ourselves. Maybe our manager's a sociopath. Maybe the long-ingrained organizational culture is one of name, blame, and shame. Maybe the focus on bottom-line results is so intense that there's no room for humanity – people are seen as interchangeable "resources", no different than the machinery and equipment running the plant. If we can't change it and it's toxic to us, the only responsible thing to do is to get out. The sooner we are able to admit that to ourselves, the sooner we can get started on a quiet job search for a healthy, sustainable workplace where we can contribute, succeed, and be valued.

- And, in the worst case scenario, where we've ignored the reality of our pain for too long and we're self-harming in any number of ways, we can leave. Even without another job to immediately go to, freed from the yoke of a toxic workplace, we can once again become the creative, resourceful, possibility thinkers we were born to be. That may not happen immediately, and we have a myriad of resources available to us in the meantime if we're open to seeing them – spouse, family, friends, neighbours, community resources, public resources … it all starts with one simple request for support.

Anna's Story

I stayed to protect the people in my department, to be a buffer between them and toxic senior managers. It was draining, crushing. It taxed my resilience to the max.

I've been a Human Resources leader for a high technology organization for several years, both watching and experiencing the wreckage created by a senior leader. My first exposure was when he started grooming an executive for the top divisional role, literally under the current leader's nose. For over a year, the leader continued to effectively deliver excellent financial returns, beyond industry norms. Eventually the individual being groomed for promotion grew impatient and threatened to leave, resulting in the division head being terminated. Unfortunately, the new guy had no experience leading a multifunctional organization, no leadership training, and no emotional intelligence. He was a hard-driving Type A, exploding in anger when anything went wrong, belittling and shaming people.

I was safe from his outbursts – I had been doing some very complex and difficult work very successfully and he needed me more than I needed him. I wasn't sheltered from the rest of it, though. He only delivered feedback through annual bonuses and Christmas party invitations, or if things went wrong. He also started to bring in some of his own people into senior roles for which they weren't qualified. And, if that wasn't bad enough, some of them were sexual harassers and yet untouchable. I was able to protect my people from them – I'd earned that by making the new CEO look exceptionally good through the work I'd done. It was a long, hard five or six months before I was offered a promotion which meant moving across the country. Ironically, he took credit for my promotion too.

He left the company about six months ago. When he took on the lead role, the division was profitable beyond industry norms. Now it's a money-losing operation. And the impact on the people: a total and utter loss of confidence and complete paralysis in terms of their freedom to act. Some good people left during his term as well. And now the new leader is gently bringing the rest out of their protective shells. And honestly, he wasn't a bad person – just unable to ask for help. A good soul, with poor impulse control, put into a job that was too big for him, with no mentorship or development. When I look back at the two years I worked for him, I see that about a third of the time I was rescuing him, a third of the time I was completely annoyed with him, and the rest of the time I was feeling sorry for him.

I was excited for the promotion – it was recognition. I was chosen as a result of doing a lot of really difficult things in a really good way and doing some really good things. I report to someone who is a complete narcissist. And he's very clever. He's promoted a toxic environment throughout his top team, setting his direct reports against each other. He is terrified of conflict and avoids tough decisions. Hence he's created a "dog eat dog" world, yet he's everyone's best friend and just can't understand why they don't all get along. And he adores the sycophants.

I'm not one of them. I call him out on his behaviours. And I pay the price. At first I thought I could change or influence him, or his behaviours, through my own behaviour. Now I know better. Now I do my work to the best of my ability but I don't try to please him. I don't seek out his feedback, or expect any warmth from him. I am careful of him after realizing he was playing mind-games with me – I'm surprised in retrospect at how easy it was for him to manipulate my thinking and my emotions. I ended up seeking therapy, which has helped.

Being brave enough to talk to others has also helped. I'd actually convinced myself that I was in the wrong at some point, having lost perspective. Being able to talk to some of my colleagues, who are also feeling the same way, has helped. And, through this process, I also realized that much

When bullying, manipulative, toxic behaviours occur in the lower ranks of management, employees can escalate complaints of abuse up their management chain or through Human Resources. They can trust that if top management only knew what was going on, action would be taken and the bad behaviours would be stopped. When the bad behaviour is happening *at* top management levels, though, employees at all levels feel powerless. What recourse is there? Perhaps an anonymous whistleblower program, or a complaint to the Board of Directors. Perhaps.

When top management is toxic, the safest course of action is to leave. RUN. Fast. And far. Don't wait for toxic behaviour to translate to poor business results and the ensuing cutbacks and layoffs. Don't wait for magic or miracles – while they may happen, they also may not. There is no neutral ground in a toxic organization. No keeping a low profile and hiding out. Choosing sides is inevitable. Choosing to be part of the toxic soup is soul-killing. Choosing to be against it is high-risk.

And yet, the risk of fighting for what's right – either overtly or covertly – is ultimately less than the risk of going along to get along. Looking out for employees' interests, preventing what harm is preventable, holding ethical ground, encouraging others to speak up … all actions that could result in job loss but protect one's integrity and one's soul.

Perhaps the most important – and most overlooked – strategy for dealing with toxic executive behaviour is the strength that is found in numbers. On any team with a toxic leader, there are members whose fear drives them to curry favour, members who choose to leave, and members who would be open to following a courageous and ethical leader with a compelling vision. Enrolling the latter group is no small task – even those wanting a better team, a better organization, have fears and seek to retain what they have, no matter how ephemeral and at risk those things are when they are ultimately at the mercy of a toxic leader. But even some small, careful and quiet action, under the radar, by a team of like-minded, ethical leaders has the potential to make a difference. Collaborative teamwork in service of what's right is a powerful force, with each act of rebellion, big or small, building a gravitational force and an energetic pull of disproportionate impact.

Mimi's Story

She told me I must be confused, that I must be remembering it wrong. But I knew I wasn't.

My manager, the head of Human Resources in a 2,500-person insurance company, had told me I was doing an excellent job and that it was such a big job she was splitting it in two and hiring a second "me". I didn't really understand why it was necessary, but she reassured me that it had nothing to do with my performance. Then I saw the job ad – not for a peer, but for a manager. And when I asked her about it, she dismissed it – and me – saying I must be confused or remembering our conversation incorrectly. I felt betrayed. I still do. This from a director who claims to support her people "100%", and who heads up HR – the "people department".

It's an example of why employees here don't trust upper management. No one is certain that they are telling us the truth, or giving us all of the information. Employees complain a lot, not to their managers, of course, but to each other. Some stop caring about their work. Many leave to go elsewhere, and no one in management seems to care that good people who do good work are leaving. Many believe that the company will fire you if you make even a small mistake - or even for no reason other than that your manager doesn't like you. People don't feel valued here, but they do feel anxious and insecure.

Professionally, it makes me very sad. I'm in an advisory position, in communications. I love my work. I am passionate about my work and about making a difference. Yet my advice is ignored. I feel like I'm not trusted by management. Since my new manager was hired, I have little work to do. I've asked for more but she doesn't like to delegate. The quality of our work has degraded too, with errors and typos in our communications. I am right there – my manager could give me work to proofread, but she doesn't. It's so frustrating.

Personally, it's very stressful. I worked for the company previously and had a really good experience. I left for a couple of years and then came back. The organization I came back to was completely different than the one I had left. There had been a merger in the meantime, and there were new leaders in the company as well. Not all of them are good managers. The manager who hired me back left two months after I rejoined. My manager is impulsive, doesn't think through the impacts of her decisions, and doesn't listen to advice. She's also treated me, and others, disrespectfully. Once she yelled at me and two of my co-workers from across the room so that others could hear. I think if you have some feedback for someone, you should take them aside and speak to them privately. I felt humiliated. And I know I'm not alone. There's bullying in our organization and no one does anything about it. Maybe it's because it's the HR director's best friend, who also works here, that is doing the bullying. People tolerate it. What else can you do? One woman complained and nothing was done. It was even implied that perhaps she deserved it.

I don't know what else I can do here. I've tried thinking positively and looking at things differently, but it's not working. I've been looking for a new job for almost two years. There aren't many corporate jobs in my region so I've expanded my search and am willing to relocate. I don't think it can get any worse where I am. I hope it won't. There's no one here to go to about any of this, nothing I can do but hope to get a new job in a better environment.

For most of us, trust takes time to build yet it can be destroyed in an instant. One casual untruth, one truth untold, one poor choice is all it takes to plant seeds of doubt which quickly grow into distrust. And once trust is broken, it is not easily rebuilt. Sometimes the wounds are so deep that it can't be rebuilt at all.

High trust organizations have a distinct advantage. The time and energy people invest in questioning, second-guessing, and verifying management's choices and directions in a low trust organization are channeled into productive, forward-moving action in a high trust organization. And trust is a two-way street. Employees feel safe taking rational risks in the interests of the business, knowing that there is fairness and process to protect them from arbitrary or extreme consequences. Managers feel safe sharing sensitive information with employees, knowing that everyone is moving – or wants to move – in the same direction.

In a low trust organization, errors are magnified. Every example of a partial-truth or what looks like an arbitrary action by management is experienced as another piece of evidence that they can't be trusted. Employees are ever-vigilant for examples that prove they're right not to trust management, and managers are equally on the lookout for evidence that employees can't be trust. It's a self-fulfilling, self-perpetuating cycle.

People can't thrive without trust. We can't be creative, take the risks necessary to stretch our comfort zone, or work collaboratively to solve problems and create opportunities if we don't have trust and if we're not trusted.

Mimi's experience reflects a number of key ways in which trust is diminished or even destroyed.

"You must be confused, or remembering it wrong."

Is there anything that cuts us to the quick as instantly as being told we're wrong about something important to us, something we know to be true? Mimi's experience of her manager telling her she must be confused or not remembering their conversation correctly is a perfect example of workplace betrayal. Leaders at all levels of an organization get to make hard decisions and then get to communicate them. It's part of the job and yet it's often the one area an otherwise effective manager falls down.

Most of us dislike conflict. It's uncomfortable and it's risky. What if we're wrong, for example? We could be publicly embarrassed. And we might have to rethink our decision in the light of new arguments. Wouldn't that cause people to question our capability and lessen our respect within the organization?

Or what if we don't have readily available – or can't share – all of the facts and information on which we based our decision? At best we'll look like we're hiding something; at worst we'll look like we made a bad decision. Besides, the corporate world is not a democracy. Why should I work so hard to get into a management position and then have to justify my decisions to employees? Which of course completely ignores the importance of the "why" behind decisions and the opportunity to enroll people if they understand what we're trying to achieve.

Even deeper, however, is our need to be liked. If I have to communicate an unpopular decision, people might not like me, and that could trigger any beliefs I might have about not being worthy. Most of us have buried our struggle to feel worthy deep down in the nether regions of our mind, which fights tooth and nail to keep it buried. Conflict can neatly and instantly drill right into the core of worthiness issues; hence, we avoid it. Even at the cost of being dishonest or disingenuous. Even at the cost of trying to convince another human being that they're wrong, their memory is faulty.

And when we're told that we're wrong, most of us immediately start to second guess ourselves. A tiny seed of self-doubt is planted, waiting to be fed and watered – which many of us are pretty good at doing. We might struggle for a time with a sense that perhaps we're going crazy: we're completely certain that we remember the initial conversation correctly, yet here is this person looking us in the eye and saying with total confidence that we're wrong. In either case, the dissonance keeps us off balance. The noise it creates in our mind distracts us long enough for us to feel that the moment to respond has passed. We're left with anger, frustration, resentment – the perfect brew to feed the beast of distrust and keep it growing.

As the level of distrust grows within the organization, people take fewer risks. They become more self-protective, sometimes even at the expense of others. In Mimi's example, people have come to tolerate workplace bullying because they know management is unwilling to take action and there's even an example where key leadership visibly took the bully's side with other employees. Why intercede then if it puts you at potential risk – particularly in a geographic region where there are few real alternative employment options?

"A few bad apples…"

Not every leader in Mimi's organization is a poor manager. In fact, it's likely that most are relatively effective. Their effectiveness, however, is overshadowed by the bad behaviour of a few key leaders. Where there is no visible consequence for behaving badly – shouting at employees, for instance - it broadens the rules for everyone. Organizational norms and expectations change with leaders' behaviour. When leaders communicate openly and honestly, keep commitments, and hold themselves and others accountable to the highest standards of ethical behaviour, those qualities permeate the organization. Conversely, when leaders tell people what they think they want to hear or are ready for, when they break commitments – or don't even realize they made a commitment – and when there's no accountability, the organization adopts those qualities.

"I love my work and I'm passionate about making a difference – but my manager doesn't give me any meaningful work to do."

Human beings have a deep-seated need for purpose and meaning. We want to make a difference. We want to leave our mark. At a minimum, we want to fill our workday with reasonably enjoyable work that provides us with the right level of challenge and satisfaction. Few people are content without enough work to do, watching the clock slowly ticking away the minutes, knowing they're being paid to do less than they're capable of and wondering how long it will be before management realizes this and they find themselves unemployed.

Managers who don't delegate effectively and who don't ensure their people are productively employed do a major disservice on a number of fronts. First, they waste the time and talents of the people who work for them – time in people's lives that they never get back. Next, they waste the resources of the organization by trying to do it all on their own. In addition to the cost of underutilized employees, none of us is capable of doing it all on our own. As Mimi's situation illustrates, at a minimum there are errors, damage is done, and rework is required. Finally, there is the insidious damage to people's souls. While it's not intentional, it's very real. Coming to work day after day, not having enough work to stay busy, not being able to stretch and grow and challenge oneself, knowing you're not contributing or making a difference … all of that takes a major toll on the human psyche. When you then factor in job insecurity and fear of job loss in a geographic region with few alternatives, the human cost is tremendous.

None of us pay that kind of cost without resentment, which is corrosive. Resentment leads to withholding our talents, our insights, our capabilities. It leads to anger and frustration which further damage workplace relationships and feed distrust. It creates pain to be numbed, often in unhealthy and unsustainable ways.

What can we do differently?

As leaders in organizations, we can:

- Tell the truth. It seems simple and straightforward and yet, how many leaders do you know who tell the truth, every time?

- Keep our commitments. First, be aware we're making a commitment – or a commitment is being registered by the other individual(s). Next, keep it. Or renegotiate it. Just don't ignore it, break it, or lie about it.

- If we step out of our integrity, own it. Admit it, apologize, and recommit.
- Hold ourselves and others accountable to high standards of behaviour. It's not enough that we're doing the right things and our team is running smoothly if the department next door is in chaos. We need to take ownership, together, for the enterprise as a whole, stepping in where necessary to ensure alignment.

- Take a firm stand and immediate action on any behaviours that look or feel like workplace bullying. Even if we personally think the target of the behaviour should have thicker skin or if they're not a top performer – the issue is what we tolerate in ourselves and each other in our workplace relations.

- Develop our people – give them stretch assignments, trust them with information and work, delegate end-to-end assignments and support and mentor them.

As employees, we can:

- Choose not to participate in the "complain-a-thon" and the endless speculation.

- Surround ourselves with as many like-minded colleagues as we can find and attract to encourage and sustain each other through honest communication and trust-based relationships.

- Identify leaders with integrity within the organization – those who while they may not have the courage of their convictions are at least behaving in ways that shelter their team members. We can explore possibilities to move into their department. In other words, we can find the least toxic – or even non-toxic – parts of the organization and do whatever it takes to move into one of them. It's difficult, if not impossible, to sustain hope and forward movement while swimming in a toxic pool. When we move to a cleaner pool – inside or outside our organization – we reopen ourselves to new possibilities and remind ourselves of who we really are. That's easy to forget while immersed in a toxic environment. And yet, it's only when we remember who we are that we do our best work and show up in the world in a way that makes a difference.

Jack's Story

Toxic: any form of excessive negativity, or an imbalance between positive and negative feelings toward an organization.

I've been here for four years. When I came here from another research and development organization, I was surprised at how many of the people here haven't worked anywhere else. They have nothing to compare to, no frame of reference other than how it's been here in the past. Frankly, the last year has been the most toxic it's ever been here. A year ago management of the organization was outsourced and a new leadership team came in.

The trade-off used to be low salaries for good pension benefits, job security, and you could get work done. Now, salaries are still low but the pension is changing, there's a funding deficit so people are anxious and afraid of losing their jobs, and the frustration level has skyrocketed.

We don't have the resources do get the job done, or the tools. Our systems don't work. Six months into the year I can't get a financial report on how my project's performing because the tools aren't functioning properly. There's huge bureaucracy and processes are convoluted. It takes months to get a new computer, equipment, business cards ... anything really. You have to make it easier for people to do their jobs – change the equation to reduce the cost of working here.

And then change it again to increase the upside. There are inequities in how people in different jobs are paid here. This is supposed to be a research and development organization, yet the people who do the research are low-paid relative to both the industry and other research organizations, and even to lower-skilled jobs here. Incentivize talented people to come work here and to stay here. Pay competitive rates.

It won't get better until the job security question is resolved. People can't work with that level of uncertainty. And the toxic people. There are some people here who take more than they give. Recently someone in a leadership position left – someone who I've experienced as disrespectful and condescending to myself and others. This wasn't a one-time incident but a sustained pattern of behaviour. He contributed to the toxicity here and it's good that he's gone.

I know that change takes time, that sometimes you need to take a step back so you can take two steps forward. Things don't change overnight and change is turbulent.

If I take an inventory of the things I hoped would change, all of them have happened or are happening. So maybe there's hope. And there are lots of good things about working here – we have a good work/life balance here, and great collaboration. We do really good work here.

And, there's always self-awareness. When I first came here, I was unbelievably frustrated. Then I had a moment of epiphany – in my frustration, I was actually contributing to the toxicity. So I got proactive. I chose to figure out solutions instead of bitching about problems. I put myself on a positive slope and with every step my attitude improved. I'm really proud of having taken things into my own hands and creating solutions, making things better. It was an important change in my way of being. Just doing something … the whole organization would benefit from doing that.

Periods of organizational change are fertile ground for toxicity to develop, or to broaden and deepen where it already exists. We resist change. It's uncomfortable, even painful. It's scary to step off into the unknown, unsure of what it means for us. A merger, acquisition, outsourcing, restructuring, or reorganization creates not only change but tremendous uncertainty.

The uncertainty created by change can trigger stress behaviours, causing both supervisors and co-workers to behave differently than they normally do – or, in some cases, to stop disguising natural, uninhibited behaviours. People can begin to interact in unhealthy ways. The most visible symptom of a workplace under stress is aggressive behaviour or workplace bullying. The leader who is normally patient starts to demonstrate visible impatience, becomes short-tempered, even loses his temper. The colleague who has always had a sarcastic sense of humour has now graduated to cynicism and even bitterness. But "fight" is only one stress response.

Flight is another. When we feel powerless, or without choice, one of the lowest-risk behaviours is withholding. Aggressive workplace behaviour carries risk of consequences, a risk which is heightened during periods of transition. A subtle withholding, on the other hand, is nearly invisible at the individual level. We may withhold effort, lowering productivity. We may withhold creativity, risk-taking, and the desire to make a contribution, lowering innovation. We may withhold feedback or ideas, increasing the risk of errors. In the extreme, we withhold our labour. That may be a relatively mild case of habitual lateness or casual absenteeism, a period of sick leave arising from stress-induced or other illness or disability, or, ultimately, leaving the organization.

When an organization experiences a long period of uncertainty, employee resilience wanes. Conditions or incidents which people typically take in stride under normal circumstances can become the catalyst for disproportionate responses. Tolerance for delays is reduced. A sense of "waiting for the other shoe to drop" sets in. New patterns of organizational behaviour emerge as employees become accustomed to developing work-arounds for dysfunctional systems and procedures. Performance expectations shift, sometimes leaving employees unsure of what's expected or how their performance will be appraised. Periodically, leadership commitments are made, often to be broken. With each successive round of unkept promises, employee trust and hope fall, until few are able to make the choice to believe. If there's a radical change resulting in new ownership, and if the transition is managed well, hope is reawakened in a larger segment of the employee population, increasing the risk of an even more significant disappointment.

As in Jack's organization, organizational change efforts tend to feel like failures part-way through, as new systems and processes are often layered on top of existing ones. There can be a tendency among new leadership teams to forge full-steam ahead, asking fewer and fewer questions over time, and working to impose what they've seen work elsewhere on the new organization. Longer service employees who participated in creating the existing procedures and systems can feel devalued as the new team dismantles the work of years. Newer employees with experience elsewhere may feel even more disillusioned through the transition period as the changes they believe will be made take too long or move in another direction. Those with low expectations of the new leadership are vindicated as failure appears imminent. Those with higher expectations can feel betrayed and even more disengaged than prior to the start of the change.

Jack's insights on leading through organizational change are sound ones. Reducing those things that demotivate employees and increasing those that motivate them are effective strategies, the specifics of which vary from one organization to another. Several, however, are common to all organizations undergoing change, including:

Acknowledge challenges with honesty and candour. Don't gloss over, downplay, or reframe them in a way employees are likely to experience as dishonest. Owning what's not working validates people, demonstrates respect, and opens the door to engaging them in problem-solving for solutions.

Engage employees. Seek first to understand – historical solutions made sense at the time they were developed and implemented, regardless of how they might appear currently to outsiders. Communicate intended outcomes clearly so that everyone understands what a good solution will look like. Then allow and encourage people to create, to experiment, to take risks in coming up with new solutions. Not only will this result in better solutions with a higher acceptance rate, but it's an opportunity to re-train employees that risk-taking and creativity are safe and valued behaviours.

Walk a mile in employee shoes. Spend time side by side with employees to understand the unwritten rules, the unacknowledged workarounds, and the day to day frustrations that get in the way. Then, tackle the issues – with tenacity and persistence. Many of them will be complex and require near-herculean efforts to fully understand and to fix. The payback is a level of trust and engagement from the workforce that can't be earned with mere talk.

Deal with toxic behaviours. People at all levels of the organization have developed habits that have been tolerated over time. Those habits and behaviours serve them in various ways they may not even consciously understand. Bullying behaviours drive short-term results, for example, as well as allowing the bully to feel in control. Often, managers avoid dealing with aggressive employees as they're unsure they will be able to deal with the behaviour effectively themselves. Cynical employees with a talent for finding the dark underside of every silver cloud often enjoy commanding an audience.

A new leadership team has a unique opportunity to role model new behaviours and to set and hold expectations for all employees, and particularly supervisors and managers. Ultimately, those unable or unwilling to change their behaviours and create new patterns need to leave the organization, ideally as soon as it becomes evident that change won't occur. This frees up energy among remaining employees who are open to change, while also demonstrating clearly to others that dysfunctional or toxic behaviours are no longer tolerated.

Over time, employees in toxic situations resulting from long periods of uncertainty and massive change can become too exhausted to be able to see possibilities or make different choices. Change can actually be easier to manage when it comes suddenly and unexpectedly, before our resilience is degraded through a lengthy wait. Some tactics for dealing with this type of toxicity include:

If you can recognize early on that a lengthy period of uncertainty is likely, take steps to protect your resilience. If you don't already practice self-care, this is the time to build that habit. Be mindful of getting enough sleep, eating well, drinking enough water, and maintaining a healthy level of physical activity as a starting point. Add a meditation or yoga practice. Spend time in nature. Connect with people you love. Have fun – whatever that looks like for you. Schedule at least one self-honouring activity a week, filling yourself back up. Increase your self-care routine as workplace stresses build over time to maintain your resilience.

Take control and make choices. Don't allow circumstances to determine your future. No one is paid to care more about your career development, for example, than you should. If your organization can no longer provide you with development opportunities, find them elsewhere. There's no rule that says only employers should pay for courses, seminars, and continuing education. Invest in yourself.

Similarly, remember that you are always at choice and there is never just one option. Intentionally making a different choice on a regular basis helps us remember that there are always multiple possibilities. Practice generating ideas and possibilities, whether you act on them or not. Brainstorm ideas with others and push your creative barriers. Training our minds to seek possibilities rather than limitations builds mental and emotional muscle.

Be prepared to make tough decisions. Ultimately, the most effective choice for you may be to leave the organization. Prepare for that possibility, even though you may never need to action it. Get your finances in order, socialize the notion with your family, and, most importantly, shift your own mindset. If you decide to leave, most likely you'll be looking for your next job. Do that from a position of empowerment and choice, not from a place of resentment and regret. Change happens – it's no one's fault and the odds are overwhelming that your next role will be an even more successful experience for you.

Kat's Story

The HR representative listened to me talk about the crushing hours I was working. The anxiety I'd developed and the medication I was on. Seeing a therapist. Asking my manager for help and being promised it but nothing changing. I waited for her response. She looked me in the eye and told me this is the corporate world. This is how it works.

She told me to "suck it up".

I was working for a small design shop when I got a call from the large consulting firm. They were looking for someone to run a design portfolio and two mutual clients had recommended me. It was an attractive job – strategic, visionary, a promotion making good use of my education and training. I met with the manager over lunch. I was also in the running for a job with a large financial institution. I decided to take whichever job I was offered first.

I took the job with the consulting firm thinking I knew what I was getting into. I'd been warned of the manager's character. A mutual client had told me I would hate working for her – but that she never stayed in one spot for long. I took the job thinking I'd outlast her. Based on what I was being told about her, I knew I could build stronger relationships and trust with client groups than she would. That would position me well for a major promotion down the road – and besides, having the consulting firm's name on my resume would open doors.

We were a small team – my manager, another manager, and myself. I was naïve – I assumed good intentions and I believed people would keep confidences. I shared too much information with my manager. She took my work and showcased it as her own. She did the same to her colleague – and caused him to lose his job. She even told me she was doing it! She wanted a promotion and he was competition. I tried to ask her questions about it – it seemed wrong to me. She told me if I didn't agree with it, I wasn't a good fit for the corporate world – that this was how it works.

It wasn't long before I started to feel overwhelmed. The volume of work was huge. I felt like I was working night and day. I was exhausted, starting to lose touch with my friends. I developed anxiety. I remember my first panic attack – I suddenly felt like I couldn't breathe, in the middle of a meeting. It was terrifying. My parents and my friends were telling me the job was killing me and asking if I was sure I wanted to do this for another year … but if this was how it worked in the corporate world, what choice did I have? Wouldn't anywhere else be the same?

That's when I went to the HR rep, who told me to "suck it up". Then she went to my manager, who'd been promoted to director, and the partner responsible for our unit and discussed me with them. My director told me to never go to HR again. She told me the partner now thought poorly of me, that any career advancement was at risk. She told me to stop talking about anxiety – or to find another job.

She started to hire more people but to do different work than I was doing. Then she told me she was looking at promoting me and hiring a junior staffer to help me, which was good news. Then the new hire came in - and introduced herself as my new manager. She made it clear that from here on in, we were doing things her way. She was just as cutthroat as my director. "Helping" me consisted of me doing all of the work I'd already been doing, and her attending meetings.

I didn't think it could get any worse, and then the director then started playing members of our growing team against each other, telling lies. Although we eventually saw what was going on, but by that time we were all fighting each other and it got to the point where work wasn't getting done and we weren't delivering on jobs.

Then I found myself in a very awkward situation. My director had outright lied to her boss, the senior partner, about her role on a project in a past life. I'd worked on the project in my former job. She pumped me for information, but then changed it when it became clear that the actual data did not support what she was recommending to the partner. One day the partner happened to ask me for the data and I gave her the valid statistics. When my director found out, she was furious.

Not long after that a colleague brought a job posting to my attention – it read like my job. My director told me it was help for me. The next day the posting had been pulled down. The following week, while she was on vacation, I was called to HR and my employment was terminated. They didn't have a reason. I was upset. The outplacement counsellor assigned to me was as shocked as I was and she helpfully provided contact information for lawyers and drove me home. Later I sent an email to the partner, thanking her for the opportunity and hoping to stay in contact in future. She responded that she was so sorry – that she had no idea I'd been let go.

It all worked out okay in the end – I had a great new job two weeks later. I get to mentor young people, students and new grads. I give them great advice so they can avoid toxic work situations. I tell them to be open and talk to their managers when things get tough. It's true that I did those things and they didn't help – maybe I could have looked harder, further … found the one person who could have helped. Found someone like me.

If I had it to do over again, the one thing I'd do differently is I would have walked out sooner. Sometimes you can't get past a bad leader. The last four or five months I worked there, I was actually thinking about committing suicide. I had no will to live, no purpose. A job almost cost me my life. It's not worth it – get out before you get to that point.

When I first heard Kat's story, I was shocked. As a lifelong HR practitioner, I've always seen my role – the role of HR – as an advocate for employees as much as a support for management. Surely we're the translators. The mediators. The compelling voice of reason and compassion for the unreasonable manager. And yet, Kat was not the only one I spoke with whose story included HR people with no empathy for the suffering employee, no words of wisdom, only a cold, corporate "suck it up" or equivalent. It's disheartening when your own profession – a profession of potential tremendous influence for good in an organization – rolls over and plays dead in service of management, both good and bad equally.

It seems to have become increasingly common for organizations to treat people – human beings – as "resources". Interchangeable units of value creation. "Talent" to be wooed, used, and discarded when the cost outweighs the value created. An employee suffering from stress and anxiety is a corporate liability, in more ways than one. While the cost of stress-related disability leaves continues to grow, the other costs are less tangible. It's the cost of having to admit to hiring a bad leader and acknowledging the damage the (s)he's caused. It's the cost of HR admitting screening and selection processes are either ineffective or not followed. It's the cost of the courage it takes to confront bad leadership, to escalate, to risk one's own job in service of the greater good. Too many HR professionals at all levels today are comfortable playing a different role, one which requires wilfully turning a blind eye to cruelty, bullying, lack of empathy. Employee complaints are treated as a symptom of entitlement – as if people paid for work aren't entitled to respect, consideration, compassion, and fair treatment.

Bad leadership at the middle management level is a failing of both HR and senior leadership. In Kat's case, the partner responsible for the unit was clearly part of the problem, changing organizational practices by mandating that new employees' mentors be their line managers rather than someone outside the business unit. She only began to ask questions of employees directly when work wasn't being delivered, missing the opportunity to keep a pulse on the unit on an ongoing basis. And even after she caught the director in either a serious error or an obvious lie, there were no repercussions. Finally, either her email response to Kat that she had no idea Kat had been let go was a lie or another missed opportunity to lead if in fact employees could be terminated without the partner's knowledge or approval.

Perhaps the greatest harm inflicted in this, and similar cases, is the perpetuation of the lie that unreasonable workloads, manipulative behaviour, and unkept promises are "what the corporate world is like". That young people coming into the workforce or being promoted into their first management role must conform or leave, which typically isn't an option. That whatever it's like in any particular instance is what it's like everywhere. This story – and it is a story – is all too often perpetuated by people who don't actually know any different. Who haven't worked outside of a single organization and have no frame of reference beyond their own "normal". It might be more accurate to tell new employees "I don't know what it's like elsewhere, but this is what it's been like here the x years I've worked here". That, at least, leaves room for the possibility that not every place of employment is equally difficult. More employees might leave toxic situations earlier if they had any reason to believe it could be better elsewhere. When their buddies and mentors – people they respect – are telling them it's the same brand of hell everywhere, where are they to turn?

As for the leader who pits team members against each other, lies, makes promises (s)he has no intention to keep … that's the leader who may only incite organizational attention when the turnover on their team is high enough. As Kat so eloquently puts it: "get out".

Employees who find themselves in toxic situations like the one Kat describes may be able to find someone in the organization who can help them. However, it's more likely that unless they are the latest in a long line of employees with a similar complaint, or they're particularly valuable to the organization, they are largely unlikely to be heard. And, just as the schoolyard bully carefully selects a victim with no voice and no allies, the most valuable employees tend not to find themselves in these situations. Bad bosses seem to have an uncanny sense of who to treat badly – or, more accurately, who they can get away with treating badly.

Kat also raises another important consideration – she was warned about the individual she would be reporting to and she chose into the situation, believing she could deal with the behaviour and outlast the manager. Once she was on the inside, however, she didn't have sufficient experience to maintain perspective or the confidence to develop and maintain healthy boundaries. Kat's naivete and lack of large organization experience would have been attractive to a predatory leader when combined with her technical expertise – the ideal employee, in many ways. Malleable. Vulnerable to manipulation. No threat. And good at her work.

Perhaps it would serve us well as a society to educate our youth on warning signs of a toxic workplace of which they should be aware:

Your manager lies, directly or by omission, or makes a habit of twisting the truth or telling half-truths.

Your manager repeatedly breaks commitments.

You can only keep up with your workload by working excessive hours on an ongoing basis – or you can't keep up with your workload even with long hours.

You start suffering from serious anxiety, panic attacks, and/or depression. If you need medication to get through your work day, you're better off finding an environment with a more manageable stress level for you.

Your manager confides in you and what they share contravenes your personal value system.

Your manager takes credit for your work.

Your manager and others in the organization repeat a mantra along the lines of "this is what the corporate world is like – you need to toughen up or get out".

The corporate world will have to start dealing with toxic leaders in a serious and systematic manner when more people do choose out of bad situations more routinely. And that's a much healthier scenario than the alternative – people struggling to get through long workdays with medication, numbing the pain of repeated betrayals, assaults on their integrity, and assaults on their mental health … or worse, people choosing out entirely.

Edward's Story

I served 25 years in the armed forces, including serving in two wars, and being responsible for a lot of people, and in all that time, I never experienced a toxic situation. A year into a new job, still within the broader public service, my manager's behaviour became so toxic that it literally triggered my latent post-traumatic stress disorder (PTSD).

The first year was great. I had a good relationship with my manager and I was doing really well – so well that he promoted me. My new role involved some long hours a lot of travel. I was a bit surprised when he told me there was no compensation for the extra hours but didn't think too much about it. Then he decided not to approve all my expenses – with an extra early start to the workday while travelling, I'd picked up a coffee and bagel rather than waiting for the hotel to start serving the complimentary breakfast. It wasn't the dollar amount that bothered me, it was the unfairness of being expected to work all kinds of extra hours without pay, travel on my own time – eating into my weekend – also without pay, and then quibbling over a few dollars for breakfast … it made no sense. It made even less sense that he approved the exact same expense for my colleague without even asking a question about it.

Our relationship grew worse over time, starting with a request I made to leave an hour early one day to go to a medical appointment. He initially refused to approve paid time. I don't know if the HR person I called to ask about the rules intervened or not, but he did approve it ultimately. I was tired of living with a different set of rules – ones he seemed to be making up especially for me – and I started to call him on it. I believe some of the events that followed were reprisal for standing up for myself.

There was the time I recognized the quality of a program I was auditing based on the content, even though it wasn't formatted the way he wanted it. He got really angry with me, but I stood my ground. Another time he sent me to a meeting way above my pay grade and tried to make me feel inadequate when I couldn't answer his extensive list of questions afterward. I knew he'd set me up to fail. I thought I could tough it out but one day I had a huge anxiety attack. I don't even remember the drive from work to the hospital, only a random thought that if the security gate was closed I would drive right through it – the need to be out of there was so overwhelming.

I should have gone off on sick leave then. The only reason I didn't was my military mindset – your job is your job and you go to work. Work became a series of anxiety attacks. I battled them silently, hiding my panic from friends and coworkers. It took everything I had to drive to work and get out of the car. I worked hard at trying to think positive thoughts, trying to distract myself from the anxiety. I did have a short time off – and I happened to look out my apartment window one afternoon only to see my manager drive by. There was no reason for him to be in my neighbourhood. I could only assume he was checking to make sure my car was in the parking lot. I don't know why – I never gave him any reason to distrust me.

Eventually a job opening came up in another department and I posted into it. I signed and returned the offer within minutes of receiving it – and it took six months before he'd release me. My first day on the new job I was scheduled to travel for a week of training. Without my saying anything, my new supervisor told me I'd be paid for my travel time and the time required to do the nightly homework. A 180 degree difference! My new manager was ex-military himself – he understood. He created a real team environment where everyone felt valued and trusted. I was sorry when he left the company. And, even though I no longer work in that department, I am still close to everyone I worked with.

My new role has had its own challenges. While things have changed for the better recently, the first year I worked with my new manager was difficult. He's made some inappropriate comments – maybe joking, but still humiliating. He's refused to help me when I've escalated work issues to him. And while he's friendly and outgoing with others, he's been visibly cold to me. Recently he started being friendlier, but honestly, I still avoid him. I don't trust him. I've applied for another job opening in a different department – I think my interview went really well. I don't want to stay in this situation – even though I take great care of myself outside of work to make sure I recharge my batteries and manage my stress, I'm still at risk.

Workplace bullies are in many ways just larger versions of schoolyard bullies, with an uncanny instinct for identifying the vulnerable. And, it's amazing just how much courage and strength those who are vulnerable demonstrate.

Our armed services personnel, along with first responders and others, experience events and take in experiences the rest of us might only see on television or in movies, or in our imaginations. Those experiences leave a mark. Many of our combat veterans return to civilian life battling post-traumatic stress disorder and yet have been conditioned to show no weakness and to apply sheer grit to keep going if that's what it takes. While these individuals appear to be among the strongest and most resilient, the truth is that they are just as vulnerable as anyone else and, in some cases even more so. Edward, for example, had not experienced his PTSD until it was triggered by workplace stress.

Edward's stress was brought on by targeted, irrational behaviours on the part of his manager. We are predisposed to look for order and structure. When someone in a leadership role behaves irrationally, treating us differently than our colleagues, for example, or ignoring the rules that are in place for everyone, we struggle with understanding that behaviour. The gulf between our expectations (rational and consistent behaviours) and our experienced reality (random and inequitable behaviours) creates a dissonance we can't reconcile. When we don't know what to expect, our anxiety levels rise. And, when we know that we can expect to be treated differently and worse than coworkers, that anxiety continues to escalate.

Managers – the layer(s) of leadership between executives and employees, whatever organizational title is used – often feel disempowered. Middle management is, in fact, one of the most challenging roles within any organization. Managers feel pressure from above to produce results and pressure from below to meet employee wishes and expectations. They have little or no opportunity to make or change "the rules", field a constant stream of demands from other areas of the organization, have limited resources, typically receive little in the way of leadership training, mentoring, and good role-modeling, are often inadequately compensated for their efforts, and are among the most vulnerable group when staffing reductions are called for. Some rise to the occasion and excel as leaders despite these circumstances. Others "quit and stay" – they do what they feel they can, reconciling themselves to a career of mediocrity, and do their best to fly under the radar screen. Some allow themselves to be in a near-constant state of resentment, either taking out their revenge on the organization through passive aggressive behaviours including withholding ideas, creativity, and problem solutions, or taking out their revenge on employees.

Almost no one sets out to be a "bad" manager. The problem is that it's easy for people to rationalize their behaviours by blaming others. At what point do we even realize we're treating one employee differently than the others? Or do we justify it with excuses and story? When an employee is experiencing powerful anxiety attacks and is determined not to allow them to show, what does that look like? It's entirely possible that if I'm focusing on managing an anxiety attack and not outwardly showing that anything is going on, I may "go blank" and appear disengaged. That can be a trigger for some people, evoking more aggressive behaviours than they might normally exhibit. There's no blame for the employee here, only an observation that when we hide what's really going on for us, how that happens to manifest can be a trigger for someone else. It doesn't excuse bad behaviour on that individual's part – particularly if they're in a position of leadership authority. It does demonstrate a lack of leadership qualities and self-management.

In some cases, managers with a particularly low emotional intelligence quotient don't realize how their behaviour impacts others. Perhaps it's because they themselves have a very high tolerance for humour at their own expense, or have been socialized to believe that everyone should be able to kid around at work and people who are "easily offended" need to toughen up. Sometimes they're simply oblivious to body language – distracted perhaps, or simply uninterested.

There are, however, instances where managers are quite conscious of the impact of their behaviours. They simply don't care, or they believe that the employee at the receiving end is deserving of disrespect or scorn, or even that shaming someone is a valid form of motivation. On some level, of course, they know what they're doing is not right – they typically don't cross the line in front of senior leaders, for example. They count on people's general fear of reprisal, reluctance to complain and/or distrust that their complaint will even be dealt with, and the shame factor. Shame may be the most disempowering emotional state. By its very definition, it implies something hidden or secret. Shame is an effective bullying tactic because it makes the target complicit. And the longer the bullying goes on, the more it becomes normalized. Witnesses to the behaviour see that there is no consequence when managers behave badly, further eroding trust in the system and discouraging complaints. Even more damaging to the organization, employees often believe that senior leadership is aware of bad management behaviours and toxic situations. Failure to act, even when it's based on genuine ignorance of what's going on cements the belief that these behaviours are tolerated. In the worst case scenario, the bad manager may achieve results personally and through his or her team which result in a promotion – a visible and tangible reward for toxic behaviours.

What can we do differently?

As leaders in organizations, we can:

- Be alert to the signals our subconscious sends us. On some level, we are always aware of the interpersonal dynamics on our team. While the workplace universe can socialize us to ignore our "spidey senses", we are irresponsible when we do so. And when we do so, out of habit or because we're uncomfortable asking challenging questions, we put someone else at risk – the employee at the receiving end of the manager's bad behaviour. And, if the situation gets serious enough, we even put ourselves at risk as courts and tribunals award increasingly larger damages to employees who have been treated badly.

- Set a very clear expectation for the organization that workplace respect is given, not earned. All employees, regardless of performance, deserve to be treated with dignity, respect, and compassion. Don't allow performance issues – real or perceived – to be an excuse for poor management behaviours.

- Be aware of employees' backgrounds and experience – if they've worked in high risk situations, such as the armed forces, be particularly watchful for behavioural changes, drops in performance, or other signals that something may be going on for them and they may need additional support.

- Be curious – when you notice something, whether it's a wrinkle in the relationship dynamic on your team or a change in behaviour or performance, have a conversation with the individual. Be curious and ask questions – then listen carefully and with an open mind for the answer. Suspend judgments and counter-arguments, and be prepared to hear information that may be uncomfortable. Then, be prepared to act on what you hear.

- Set clear leadership expectations up front and reiterate and clarify them regularly. And don't forget to walk the talk – as a senior leader, we set the tone and example. When you do run across an example of bad management behaviours or practices, deal with it – immediately and decisively. That means setting clear expectations and providing meaningful consequences where warranted. It also means being smart about who is promoted or hired into supervisory positions and, sometimes, removing those who may be technically strong but abuse or misuse their power and their people.

As employees, we can:

- Seek medical assistance when we need it and take care of ourselves – that means taking the time we need and getting the care we need to be or get well.

- Avoid isolating ourselves – whether we have a support network at work, outside of work, or both, we need people we trust and in whom we can confide. They can serve not only as moral support and comfort, but also a sounding board when we start to lose perspective on our manager's behaviour.

- Escalate issues and request organizational support when we're being treated poorly – with one caveat. If the organization genuinely tolerates bad behaviours and fosters a culture of "get tough or get out", then the healthiest choice is to find work elsewhere. While that can be scary – all too often we believe we'll never find an equivalent job – and it can feel unfair – if we're the one being victimized, why should we have to leave? – it's better to protect our mental, physical, and emotional health than to be in the right and unwell.

- Be open to support and assistance – if someone in the organization you feel you can trust reaches out to you with curiosity and an offer of support, be open to it. Many of us are accustomed to doing it on our own and even believe that asking for or receiving support is a sign of weakness. Those perspectives don't always serve us well. When it comes to an abusive manager or a toxic workplace environment, there's strength in numbers. Leverage like-minded individuals and influencers.

Ellen's Story

I told them "We wouldn't be having these meetings if I'd broken an ankle." I went from being a capable employee to someone they had to micromanage. And there was no coming back from that; I never felt that they saw me as capable again.

It actually started out well – I had made the move from private practice to public health smoothly. Working in schools and with social service programs felt so much more aligned to my values, and I still had the opportunity to do the job I loved and to fully utilize my skills and experience. The first year and a half or so, I even mentored my supervisor, another healthcare professional but with less breadth of experience than I had at the time.

The challenge started when I was promoted to more of a desk job managing a care plan. I missed going out to the schools and interacting with people in person – particularly the kids. And, being in the office all the time, I had no respite from my supervisor. Our really positive relationship of the first 18 months I had been there shifted after a while. She became very controlling, micromanaging us and withholding information. She was passive aggressive and manipulative.

I started noticing changes in my health. I had a constant headache, I felt teary all the time, and I wasn't sleeping. When I finally saw my doctor, my blood pressure was sky-high as well. She thought I was depressed and prescribed time off. She also wanted support in managing my health, but in this area the only way to get to see a psychiatrist was to be admitted to the acute mental health unit. I was admitted and stayed there for five days during which a couple of coworkers I was close to came to visit me.

Taking time off didn't go over well at work, despite the fact that I'd had very little time off in the previous eight or nine years. My supervisor had always been a bit nosy and now she kicked into overdrive. She was so persistent in questioning one of my coworkers about the medical reason for my absence that he eventually cracked – he called me one day, nearly in tears, to confess that she'd worn him down and he'd told her it was depression. That started a lengthy cycle of what I can only describe as harassment. She called me at home every two or three days to ask me when I was coming back to work. Every time the phone rang, I flinched. And when I saw it was the office, I felt every part of me clench up with anxiety. It didn't stop until my sister happened to pick up the phone one day and threatened to hire a lawyer and file a lawsuit if the harassment didn't stop.

After just under a year of leave, with counselling and medication and training under my belt, it was time to go back to work. The care program I'd been running had ended and I was happy to be going back to my work visiting schools – work I loved.

As a condition of my return, my employer asked for an independent psychiatric assessment – even though the only way they could have known it was a mental health issue was from my supervisor's prying. When my union refused to agree to one, they admitted that they wanted to be certain I wouldn't pose a danger to the children. Just hearing that was devastating to me. Although I didn't have to go for the assessment, there was a return to work program put in place and it was awful.

Every week I met with three managers, including my supervisor, my union representative, and counsellor the group insurance carrier had assigned to my case. The week I was scheduled to return to my school visits they announced that instead of having the usual healthcare assistant with me, a manager would accompany me. Despite their protestation that this was something they did periodically, I'd never seen it or heard of it in the years I'd worked there. I felt targeted and I spoke up, telling them it didn't feel right and that it felt like it was only happening because I was returning to work after a mental rather than a physical disability leave. They remained adamant that it would happen and suggested my coworkers didn't want to work with me – another emotional blow. I remember leaving the meeting and feeling so sick inside that I threw up in a snowbank just outside the building.

I reached out that week to someone in the national union who specialized in Human Rights advocacy. She listened to my story and agreed to come to the next weekly meeting. I'm glad she was there – after listening quietly throughout the meeting, she articulated what I was feeling: this was a poisonous workplace and it was making me suffer. Even though the HR manager was dismissive of her intent to bring suit, I felt validated coming out of that meeting. Someone had heard me at last. Someone had seen what was happening to me and was willing to speak up for me.

It didn't make a difference, things didn't improve. I struggled for the next five years. My medication wasn't right and I was overmedicated, lethargic and sleeping too much. I started being late for work, a lot. I couldn't admit it at the time – I probably couldn't even really see it then – but I didn't want to go to work. I didn't want to face the questions – "Is your depression bothering you? They had no idea what it was like. It wasn't even just work. When I'd sprained my ankle badly a few years earlier, my neighbours couldn't do enough to help me. When I was off with depression, all but one of them virtually shunned me. Even my sister couldn't really understand why I didn't just get on with it. It's a lonely place, depression.

And the longer it went on, the worse I felt. My performance reviews were mixed during those years. I got really good reviews on my work, the actual job, but the comments about me were rough. My supervisor described me as too emotional, too sensitive, too soft. I knew they saw me as weak and I was seeing myself as weak. Over time, I became passively suicidal. I wasn't ready to take my own life, but I knew if I was diagnosed with a potentially terminal illness, I would not have sought treatment. I thought about being hit by a truck … eventually my doctor referred me to another psychiatrist.

He saved my life. He spent time with me, asked questions and listened to understand. He prescribed new medication that actually worked. I started him that fall and when my daughter came home from university for Christmas she asked me who I was and what I'd done with her mother, the difference was so noticeable. I saw him for a total of seven years and when I thanked him at our last appointment and told him he'd saved my life, he told me "we" had saved my life, together. That I'd done the heavy lifting.

And I had. During that time I reached a point where I was tired of the bullshit at work. I ran for union president and won, holding the office for five years and through two rounds of tough collective bargaining. It may have made me even more of a target for management. I received multiple disciplinary letters and unpaid suspensions, even for incidents where I wasn't at fault. What was even worse than the discipline was the approach. One time I was coming back from vacation and there was a massive storm which stranded our flight. As a result, I couldn't make it in to work on the Monday and when I called my supervisor to explain, she played a mind game with me, asking how I was going to report the time on my timesheet and then declining all of the paid leave options available to me, one at a time. I was disciplined for being away from work without permission and given a five day unpaid suspension and yet another threat of dismissal. It was exhausting and emotionally draining.

Another, similar, incident became the final straw. My family circled the wagons and refused to stand by and watch me suffer any longer. At their urging, I went back to the doctor and ended up being off for almost a year again. I felt broken, unbearably anxious all the time. The sound of an office door closing behind me, the often-innocent "do you have a minute?", created so much panic and apprehension inside me that when it turned out to be a work-related question, I found myself being effusively friendly and helpful out of sheer relief.

And worst of all, the job I had loved so much had soured. I no longer wanted to do it. I wanted out and ultimately, with help, I found it. I decided to go back to school and retrain for a different career. Terrifying at age 52 and still suffering from years of feeling weak and incapable. But strong enough to want to live. And supported by my husband, my daughter, my sister, and my healthcare team.

Boy, did it feel good to resign. I turned up at the office unexpectedly and I could see my resignation caught my supervisor entirely off-guard. She was expecting me to come back to work and here I was talking a stand for myself one last time, getting out from under her passive aggressive, controlling ways. And it still feels good. I love my new job. It's my life purpose, what I was always meant to do. I get up joyfully each morning to go to work and I come home feeling fulfilled. My coworkers are terrific, our clients are amazing. I'm happy. Really happy. And after five years, I can finally drive past that place and not feel upset.

It's often impossible to determine the precise origin of a mental health battle, just as many physical health battles remain a mystery. We're holistic beings and our professional and personal lives intersect and interact. While it's unlikely workplace stresses and toxicity alone can cause depression and other mental health issues in individuals who are not already predisposed, they certainly worsen anything that may already be playing out and they can be the tipping point beyond which an individual can no longer cope effectively.

Perhaps even worse, the stigma still associated with mental health issues literally feeds the cycle of ill health. Physical issues are more tangible. We tend to trust the medical evidence in support of physical health issues more than those relative to mental health. To many, mental health issues seem subjective. We've all experienced physical pain on some level and so we can all relate to it. Medical science can explain heart disease, cancer, diabetes, and other acute and chronic physical issues clearly, and provide objective empirical evidence of them and of recovery from them. Mental health – less so.

How our mind works, even how our brain works, is still not nearly as well understood. Advances in thinking and research are published regularly – for example, there's a growing body of evidence that gut health is closely linked to depression. It may be that in the future, for some individuals, prebiotics will became a powerful component in the medication toolkit to battle depression. In the meantime, however, there seems to be as much speculative science as there is hard science in this area, and that makes it easier to discount the whole area of mental health.

More critically, though, mental health - or the absence of it – frightens many of us. We can make the link between smoking and lung cancer and we can choose not to smoke or be in close proximity to someone who is smoking. We may or may not buy the link between stress and mental health and, even if we do, we may not see that we have a choice other than stress. If I'm to accept that high levels of stress can lead to mental health issues and I also believe I can't avoid high levels of stress, then that's a lose-lose proposition. Stress is ubiquitous in our lives today and many of us have not found, or are simply not using, the tools to manage it effectively. So the easier resolution of the conundrum is to deny, or to qualify, the link between stress and mental health. And the easiest way to protect ourselves is to blame the victim – to decide there's something wrong with people who succumb to depression or suffer from anxiety, or that it's a choice they're making.

Ellen speaks eloquently of being treated as "weak" and feeling weak. To an objective observer, her ability to remain at work for long periods of time despite her health challenges and the toxic environment created by her supervisor's behaviour, and even to challenge authority withiin that environment, speaks of her strength, courage, and resilience. Yet, her experienced reality was that she was weak and she was seen as weak – and as incapable. It may have been easier for Ellen's supervisor and others to choose to see her as weak – after all, if she was strong, like them, then they too would be vulnerable to becoming ill. If she was somehow different from them, then they could feel safer.

The problem with labelling someone as different, or weak, or incapable, is that as soon as we do that, we begin to treat them that way, whether we intend to or not. Even in a non-toxic, neutral, or downright supportive work environment, that can create a problem. Here's our co-worker, back from a leave resulting from a mental health issue. Even if that individual isn't perceived as weak or somehow defective, we may, consciously or otherwise, treat them as requiring special handling. We speak more softly to them and around them. We avoid certain subjects, deciding on their behalf that they may not be able to handle them. We are quicker to notice changes in their demeanor and to attach meaning to them. That carefulness in and of itself, while it can be well-intentioned, is harmful in that it holds the individual incapable.

Mental health issues can pose even more complex challenges in workplaces. In Ellen's case, it's not entirely unreasonable that her employer would have requested an independent or third-party psychiatric assessment on her return to work, or provided extra supervision, given that she was working with children. The request might have been a sound risk mitigation strategy to manage potential legal liabilities.

However, a potentially reasonable request – or at least one understandable from a legal risk perspective – takes on an entirely different colouration within a toxic workplace environment. Had Ellen's supervisor not inappropriately pried her health information out of a coworker, the organization would not have known (and were not legally entitled to know) that she was dealing with a mental health issue. They would not have made the request. Even if they had been entitled to the information, given that the supervisor's behaviours were a major contributor to Ellen's illness before her leave and continued during her leave with the regular phone calls, it's difficult to envision that the request could have been made in a positive manner. Given the context, the request could only make Ellen feel even less trusted and capable.

Ellen's case is a powerful example of a toxic cycle: a toxic leader creates a workplace environment that results in or exacerbates an existing mental health issue, which the organization is then incapable of managing effectively, resulting in an even more toxic work environment and greater suffering for the individual.

What can we do differently?

As leaders in organizations, we can:

- Recognize and intervene when supervisors or managers are demonstrating toxic behaviours, being particularly sensitive to performance situations. Ineffective managers sometimes use real or perceived performance issues or workplace behaviours as a rationale to micromanage employees or treat them differently, and with less compassion, than other employees.

- Be sensitive to changes in employee behaviour. As leaders, we have a responsibility to notice what's going on for our people. When someone whose performance has been exemplary suddenly starts demonstrating unusual behaviours, it's time to get curious, in a respectful way. In a unionized workplace, there's a perfect opportunity to work collaboratively with the union to support an individual. Many workplaces today have an Employee Assistance

Program or can access advice and support through their group benefits provider. Even local community resources can be a source of information and guidance. Obviously, protecting an individual's privacy and respecting healthy boundaries is a prime concern – but so is ensuring that someone who is going through a challenging time has access to assistance and support, and knows that they are valued.

- In addition to respecting and valuing the individual, it's important that we avoid thinking of someone as being less than capable, or treating them as if they were.

- Finally, there is now a range of workplace wellness programs available to educate and support leaders and employees in dealing with mental health issues in the workplace. There is no longer an excuse for pleading ignorance or for behaving as if depression, anxiety, and other mental health issues are not real or somehow don't belong in the workplace. All of us bring our whole selves to work – we don't leave our stresses and anxieties at home, any more than we can leave the stresses and strains of a toxic workplace behind when we head out at the door at the end of the day. Every workplace today needs to be as well equipped to manage mental health as we are at managing physical health issues.

As employees, we can:

- Acknowledge how we're really feeling, including when all the positive thinking techniques we've learned aren't having an impact. Lean into our emotions and allow ourselves to process them. Anger, sadness, disappointment … whatever we're feeling is processed in our bodies in 30 seconds to three minutes when we lean into them fully. If that's not working, it may be something more serious and it's vital that we seek help.

- Utilize all the resources at our disposal – seek professional assistance, keep our medical team advised of what's working and what's not, be open to changes in medication, ask plenty of questions, and follow medical advice. And, if it continues to be ineffective, get a second opinion. Or a third. Do whatever it takes to recover our health and be well.

- If it's a coworker, a family member, a friend, or a neighbour who needs support, provide it. Don't back away from someone whose behaviour has changed – lean in and offer assistance. Don't avoid or shun someone who shares that they're battling a mental illness (or a physical one for that matter) – let them know you care about them, ask them what kind of support would serve them, and provide it. Educate yourself so that you can provide support effectively.

- Recognize when a supervisor or manager's behaviour at work is pushing past healthy boundaries and take appropriate measures. Sometimes that's a direct conversation being clear with our own boundaries. Sometimes it's third party intervention – a union rep, an HR rep, a mediator … whoever is available, in a position to have influence, and is open to helping. Sometimes it's a formal complaint or grievance. In the most extreme case, it may be a decision to leave the workplace, whether temporarily or permanently.

Mental health in the workplace is a subject that still makes many people uncomfortable. That's not entirely surprising – many people still feel uncomfortable and unsure of how to be supportive when it's a physical health issue. Being uncomfortable is not an excuse to do nothing, or to behave badly or insensitively. Whether there is an increase in mental health issues or simply a greater openness and willingness to disclose them, sooner or later all of us will be faced with a choice. Being prepared – or at the very least being open – can make all the difference.

What We Can Do as Leaders

What We Can Do as Leaders

Coach our people to strive for equilibrium in their lives and role model balance. That means conducting business largely within normal business hours, avoiding email and telephone requests and assignments outside of working hours where possible.

Notice dysfunctional or unsustainable work habits and patterns and get curious. Support employees in maintaining sustainable work habits to avoid burnout.

Acknowledge and celebrate successes, large and small, so that employees feel seen and valued. Pay particular attention to and highlight results created without heroic sacrifices to encourage healthy, sustainable work habits even while focusing on results. Hold people accountable for results – successes and failures – without focusing exclusively or excessively on failures.

Support employees in using experiences of not achieving what they committed to as **learning opportunities**, rather than seeing them as failures. Probe with open-ended questions.

Take the time to understand the level of effort required to achieve results so we can **acknowledge the contribution** – and the sacrifices – our people are making.

Identify high priority results and activities – avoid making everything equally important (and, therefore, equally unimportant).

Pay attention to employees and their wellbeing. Watch for changes in their manner or behaviour and get curious when we see new behaviours.

Be alert to the signals our subconscious sends us about our employees and about relationships between employees.

Know what motivates and what demotivates our people and strive to ensure their jobs have a healthy balance.

Ask people, regularly, what support they need – normalize the idea that no one is an island and it's okay to ask for support. Model asking for support.

Create safe opportunities for people to share their experiences and insights, to deepen their learning and to share it across the team.

Create opportunities for flexible workplace strategies to support people's best efforts – allow "morning people" to start work earlier, respect daycare deadlines, enable people to opt for non-peak commute times.

When our own leader is toxic, quietly **garner support from colleagues** to take action – whether it's simply a quiet defence of the most vulnerable or an appeal to higher powers for intervention, or something in between.

Tell the truth. Every time. Even when it's unpalatable or unwelcome, it's still easier for people to deal with than lies or evasion.

Acknowledge challenges with honesty and candour.

During times of change in particular, **engage employees in finding solutions.**

Walk a mile in employee shoes, especially in a change situation, to build empathy for what it feels like to be on the frontline.

Keep commitments – be aware when we're making a commitment (intended or not) and keep it or renegotiate it.

Own mistakes, acknowledge them, apologize, recommit to something different.

Hold ourselves and others accountable to high standards of behaviours and strive for alignment.

Take a firm stand and immediate action on any behaviours that look or feel like workplace bullying. That also includes be on the watch for it.

Develop our people – give them stretch assignments, trust them, delegate, support, and coach and mentor. As leaders, the most effective contribution we can make to our organizations is to grow more and better leaders.

Set a clear and non-negotiable expectation that workplace respect is given, not earned. All employees, regardless of performance, deserve to be treated with dignity, respect, and compassion. Never allow performance issues (real or perceived) to be an excuse for poor management behaviours.

Be aware of employees' backgrounds and experience. If they've worked in high risk situations, such as the armed services or as first responders, be particularly watchful for behavioural changes, drops in performance, or other signals that something may be going on for them and they may need additional support.

Be curious – when you notice something, have a conversation with the individual. Ask questions, then listen carefully and with an open mind for the answer. Suspend judgments and counter-arguments, and be prepared to hear something uncomfortable. And, be prepared to act on it.

Set clear leadership expectations up front and reiterate and clarity them regularly.

Walk the talk – set the tone and be the example.

Recognize and intervene when supervisors or managers are demonstrating toxic behaviours, being particularly sensitive to performance situations. Ineffective managers sometimes use real or perceived performance issues or workplace behaviours as a rationale to micromanage employees or treat them differently, and with less compassion, than other employees.

Be sensitive to changes in employee behaviour. As leaders, we have a responsibility to notice what's going on for our people. When someone whose performance has been exemplary suddenly starts demonstrating unusual behaviours, it's time to get curious, in a respectful way. In a unionized workplace, there's a perfect opportunity to work collaboratively with the union to support an individual. Many workplaces today have an Employee Assistance Program or can access advice and support through their group benefits provider. Even local community resources can be a source of information and guidance. Obviously, protecting an individual's privacy and respecting healthy boundaries is a prime concern – but so is ensuring that someone who is going through a challenging time has access to assistance and support, and knows that they are valued.

In addition to respecting and valuing the individual, it's important that we **avoid thinking of someone as being less than capable**, or treating them as if they were.

Finally, there is now a range of **workplace wellness programs** available to educate and support leaders and employees in dealing with mental health issues in the workplace. There is no longer an excuse for pleading ignorance or for behaving as if depression, anxiety, and other mental health issues are not real or somehow don't belong in the workplace. All of us bring our whole selves to work – we don't leave our stresses and anxieties at home, any more than we can leave the stresses and strains of a toxic workplace behind when we head out at the door at the end of the day. Every workplace today needs to be as well equipped to manage mental health as we are at managing physical health issues.

What We Can Do As Employees

What We Can Do As Employees

Seek self-awareness. Recognize our own pitfalls and avoid the traps we routinely fall into. Avoid working in situations and for and with people who trigger dysfunctional behaviours in us.

Know our own warning signs so we can recognize when we're heading for overload or burnout – and, when we recognize it, change it. Do something different. Seek support and assistance.

Practice good self-care activities on a regular basis – eat right, get enough exercise, get the right amount of sleep for your needs, spend time outdoors, spend time with people who energize us, meditate, do yoga, be mindful, breathe deeply, have fun, make time for social activities, get a massage … know what restores and refreshes you and then DO IT.

Avoid participating in group complaining and whining … it doesn't change anything.

Surround ourselves with like-minded colleagues and sustain each other through honest communication and trust-based relationships.

Identify leaders with integrity within the organization and find ways to move from a toxic situation to a less or non-toxic situations.

Take ownership for our choices. Be responsible. Then, make a different, more effective choice. Avoid falling into the trap of seeing ourselves as the victim. Victims are powerless – people who make choices, even bad ones, are at least empowered and can choose differently.

Look for possibilities – even when we don't believe they exist. There are always possibilities but if we don't look, we won't see them.

Ask for what we need or want without assuming we can't have it – sometimes we create our own limitations out of fear of asking. If we don't ask, the outcome is always a "no". Asking creates possibility.

Take stock of our personal values and make choices in accordance with them, accepting the consequences of those choices.

Be radically honest with ourselves when we're in a situation we can't detoxify and start looking for alternative employment. Or, just leave. Our health, our safety, our very lives are more important than any paycheque.

Watch for signs of toxicity – lies, half-truths, broken commitments, excessive workload and demands on an ongoing basis, breaches of your values and integrity, others taking credit for your work, starting to experience stress, anxiety, depression, panic attacks, and health issues resulting from your workplace, and a management mantra of "this is what it is … toughen up or get out" or any variation thereof. Choose out.

Recognize when we can't deal with prolonged uncertainty and take steps to **protect our resilience**. Take control and make our own choices, being prepared to make tough decisions.

Seek assistance when we need it and **avoid isolating ourselves**. Build, maintain, and lean into our support network.

Escalate issues and request organizational support when we're being treated poorly.

Acknowledge how we're really feeling, including when all the positive thinking techniques we've learned aren't having an impact. Lean into our emotions and allow ourselves to process them. Anger, sadness, disappointment … whatever we're feeling is processed in our bodies in 30 seconds to three minutes when we lean into them fully. If that's not working, it may be something more serious and it's vital that we seek help.

Utilize all the resources at our disposal – seek professional assistance, keep our medical team advised of what's working and what's not, be open to changes in medication, ask plenty of questions, and follow medical advice. And, if it continues to be ineffective, get a second opinion. Or a third. Do whatever it takes to recover our health and be well.

If it's a coworker, a family member, a friend, or a neighbour who needs support, provide it. Don't back away from someone whose behaviour has changed – **lean in and offer assistance**. Don't avoid or shun someone who shares that they're battling a mental illness (or a physical one for that matter) – let them know you care about them, ask them what kind of support would serve them, and provide it. Educate yourself so that you can provide support effectively.

Recognize when a supervisor or manager's behaviour at work is pushing past healthy boundaries and take appropriate measures. Sometimes that's a direct conversation being clear with our own boundaries. Sometimes it's third party intervention – a union rep, an HR rep, a mediator ... whoever is available, in a position to have influence, and is open to helping. Sometimes it's a formal complaint or grievance. In the most extreme case, it may be a decision to leave the workplace, whether temporarily or permanently.

To Sum It Up …

To Sum It Up ...

Many of us have a compulsive approach to work. We put our work at the centre of our lives. We build our identities and worth around it. We sacrifice time with our spouse or partner, children, extended family, and friends, to meet work deadlines.

Sometimes that's an effective strategy. Sometimes it's not. The trick is to recognize when we're making choices that serve us and when we're making choices that don't.

What <u>never</u> serves us, however, is choosing to remain immersed in a toxic workplace. It's time. We get to embrace our own value and worth and to create change. Whether that's effecting change in a toxic workplace through any of the myriad of strategies and tactics outlined in this book and elsewhere, or choosing out of a toxic workplace.

If your workplace is toxic and you're suffering the effects, I have three words for you: choose and move.

About the Author

I am:

A worthy, valuable, joyful, and powerful woman.

A certified life coach, team coach, executive coach, and workshop facilitator.

A certified Laughter Yoga instructor!

Certified in coaching, NLP and NLP coaching, Create Your Future Coaching/Time Line Therapy, and Hypnotherapy.

A career Human Resources professional and senior executive.

A wife, mother, dog-mom, friend, boss, employee.

Passionate about transformation – personal, group, workplace.

Enough.

With love and inspiration,

Esther Zdolec

www.heart-goals.com

esther@heart-goals.com

estherzdolec@yahoo.com

www.ingramcontent.com/pod-product-compliance
Lightning Source LLC
Chambersburg PA
CBHW061444180526
45170CB00004B/1552